Great
American
SPORTS
HEROES

270 of the
greatest
QUOTES
about sports

SUCCESSORIES
LIBRARY

Dedication

*This book is dedicated
with love to my stepfather
Richard Crisorio*

*Compiled by: Peggy Anderson
Edited by: Kyle Miller
Book Design: Tim McGovern and Eric Zeigler
Photography: Kenji Kerins Photography
Illustrations: Rick Gonnella*

ISBN: 1-880461-32-3

1 2 3 4 5 6 7 8 Printing/AK/Year 98 97 96 95 94

Great American SPORTS HEROES

270 of the greatest QUOTES about sports

Contents

Joe Frazier
Heavyweight Boxer

"Kill the body and

the head will die."

Bobby Locke
PGA Golfer

"Drive for show.

But putt for dough."

Henry Aaron
Major League Outfielder

"I don't want them

to forget Ruth. I

just want them to

remember me!"

Chris Evert
1954 –

The consistency of her performance and her steady baseline play made Chris Evert one of the most successful women in professional tennis. She won at least one major singles championship every year for thirteen consecutive years, a record. An exemplary professional in her relations with her colleagues, the press and the public, she was the first player to win 1,000 singles matches as well as 150 tournaments, and the first woman to earn one million dollars in prize money. Her winning percentage, .8996, is the highest in the history of professional tennis.

"If you can react the same way to winning and losing, that's a big accomplishment. That quality is important because it stays with you the rest of your life, and there's going to be a life after tennis that's a lot longer than your tennis life."

"Ninety percent of my game is mental. It's my concentration that has gotten me this far."

"Every time, all the time, I'm a perfectionist. I feel I should never lose."

3

4

Earl Campbell
NFL Fullback

"Somebody will always break your records. It is how you live that counts."

Annie Dillard
Writer

"A baseball weighted your hand just so, and fit it. Its red stitches, its good leather and hardness like skin over bone, seemed to call forth a skill both easy and precise."

Philip K. Wrigley
Owner, Chicago Cubs

"Baseball is too much of a sport to be called a business, and too much of a business to be called a sport."

Samuel Johnson
Essayist & Writer

"Golf — a game in which you claim the privileges of age, and retain the playthings of childhood."

Mike Singletary
NFL Linebacker

"Do you know what my favorite part of the games is? The opportunity to play. It is as simple as that. God, I love that opportunity."

Satchel Paige
Major League Pitcher

"I never threw an illegal pitch. The trouble is, once in a while I toss one that ain't never been seen by this generation."

"One important key to success is self-confidence. An important key to self-confidence is preparation."

"Sports and politics do mix. Behind the scenes, the two are as inextricably interwoven as any two issues can be."

"If it had not been for the wind in my face, I wouldn't be able to fly at all."

Arthur Ashe

1943 – 1993

A man of enormous character and courage, Arthur Ashe established a record in 1968 that may never be equaled in the world of tennis, winning both the Amateur and U.S. Open championships. With a commanding serve-and-volley game, he became a dominating presence on the courts. For twelve years he was in the World Top Ten, and for fourteen years he was in the U.S. Top Ten. He was the first black man to win a U.S. championship and Wimbledon, and the first U.S. tennis player to earn $100,000 in a single season. Ashe wrote a comprehensive book on black sports history, *Hard Road to Glory*, and played a dominant role in the resurgence of the American Davis Cup, both as a player and as team captain.

Frank Gifford
NFL Halfback

"Pro football is like nuclear warfare. There are no winners, only survivors."

John F. Kennedy
35th President of the United States

"We are inclined to think that if we watch a football game or a baseball game, we have taken part in it."

Don Marquis
Writer

"Fishing is a delusion entirely surrounded by liars in old clothes."

Edna Ferber
Writer

"Any man who can look handsome in a dirty baseball suit is an Adonis."

Paul Westphal
NBA Guard and Coach

"The key to any game is to use your strengths and hide your weaknesses."

Frank Layden
NBA Coach

"When I was coaching, the one thought that I would try to get across to my players was that everything I do each day, everything I say, I must first think what effect it will have on everyone concerned."

Ted Williams

1918 –

Often ignored by the press during his remarkable career, today Ted Williams stands as one of the finest hitters to ever play the game of baseball. He missed three years during his prime serving in World War II and another two seasons to the Korean War, yet still managed to complete his career with a .344 lifetime batting average, 521 home runs and a .634 slugging percentage. His concentration at the plate was legendary, his batting eye unerring. As proof of his abilities, in 1957, at the age of thirty-nine, he batted .388 to lead the league, and hit thirty-eight home runs. The next year, his .328 average led the league again. In all, he captured six batting titles, four home run championships, led the American League in slugging percentage nine different times and captured two Triple Crowns.

"All I want out of life is that when I walk down the street, folks will say, 'There goes the greatest hitter who ever lived.'"

"I always did my best when I realized the assignment was going to be difficult. From there, my attitude was better, more serious, and I got down to the job of preparing myself better than if I thought it was going to be easy."

"I'd rather swing a bat than do anything else in the world."

Cotton Fitzsimmons
NBA Coach

"I have a basic philosophy that I've tried to follow during my coaching career. Whether you're winning or losing, it is important to always be yourself. You can't change because of the circumstances around you."

Bob Plager
NHL Coach
(reflecting on the Toronto Maple Leafs)

"Coaching that team is like having a window seat on the Hindenberg."

Earvin "Magic" Johnson
NBA Guard

"Even when I went to the playground, I never picked the best players. I picked guys with less talent, but who were willing to work hard, who had the desire to be great."

Roger Maris
Major League Outfielder

"You hit home runs not by chance, but by preparation."

Roger Staubach
NFL Quarterback and
Sports Broadcaster

"Nothing good comes in life or athletics unless a lot of hard work has preceded the effort. Only temporary success is achieved by taking short cuts."

Jack Lemmon
Actor

"If you think it's hard to meet new people, try picking up the wrong golf ball."

14

"I'm not mean at all. I just try to protect myself. You'll see I don't ever pick on anybody who has a number above 30."

"If you are determined enough and willing to pay the price, you can get it done."

"I don't think anything is unrealistic if you believe you can do it."

Mike Ditka

1939 –

According to some experts he was the perfect player — an unparalleled blocker, a driving runner and a sure-handed receiver. Rookie of the Year in 1961, he led the Chicago Bears to their first NFL title in seventeen years, making game-winning catches throughout a brilliant season. In 1971 as a Dallas Cowboy, he scored the decisive touchdown in Super Bowl VI. As a head coach, he led the Chicago Bears to a near-perfect 17-1 season in 1985 and a decisive victory in Super Bowl XX. He was inducted into the Pro Football Hall of Fame in 1988.

Sir Edmund Hillary
Mountain Climber

"You don't have to be a fantastic hero to do certain things — to compete. You can be just an ordinary chap, sufficiently motivated to reach challenging goals."

Roger Kahn
Writer

"You may glory in a team triumphant, but you fall in love with a team in defeat."

John Madden
NFL Coach and
Sports Broadcaster

"The only yardstick for success our society has is being a champion. No one remembers anything else."

Ty Cobb
Major League Outfielder

"I had to be first all the time — first in everything. All I ever thought about was winning."

A. J. Foyt
Race Car Driver

"You get out in front — you stay out in front."

Terry Bradshaw
NFL Quarterback and Sports Broadcaster

"When you've got something to prove, there's nothing greater than a challenge."

Arnold Palmer

1929 –

When he charged the fairways with his special brand of spirited enthusiasm, Arnold Palmer single-handedly awakened the American public to the world of golf. Though anything but a textbook player, his powerful stroke and determined focus captivated the imagination of men and women throughout the country. Palmer first made his presence known with a victory in the 1954 U.S. Amateur competition. Four years later, as a professional, he captured the first of his four Masters titles. Trailing by seven strokes at the start of the final round of play, he scored a miraculous come-from-behind victory by birdieing six of the first seven holes and shooting a 30 on the front nine. Palmer won sixty tournaments on the PGA Tour, including a victory at the Canadian PGA at the age of fifty-one.

"I've always made a total effort, even when the odds seemed entirely against me."

"I play to win, everybody knows I play to win."

"I never quit trying. I never felt that I didn't have a chance to win."

19

Bruce Jenner
Decathlete and
Olympic Gold Medalist

"What does a fellow

compete for anyway?

A gold medal?

Money? Glory?

No, it's fulfillment."

Henry Aaron
Major League Outfielder

"Girls excel at

basketball, golf and

tennis, and there is

no logical reason

they shouldn't

play baseball."

Earl Campbell
NFL Fullback

"If it weren't for

the dark days, we

wouldn't know

what it is to walk

in the light."

John Lowenstein
Major League Outfielder

"They should move first base back a step to eliminate all the close plays."

Will Rogers
Humorist

"The income tax has made liars out of more Americans than golf."

Lou Holtz
Head Coach,
University of Notre Dame

"The man who complains about the way the ball bounces is likely the one who dropped it."

"There has always been something new, demanding and testing every day I play. I love the challenge."

"When I had to give up swimming because it wasn't good for my golfing muscles, I began to think of what else I would have to sacrifice if I wanted to keep playing golf."

"The pressure makes me more intent about each shot."

Nancy Lopez

1957 –

During her first full season on the Ladies
Professional Golf Association Tour in
1978, Nancy Lopez won nine
tournaments, including a record five in
a row. She garnered Rookie of the Year
honors for her exceptional play,
collecting the Vare Trophy as well
for the best tournament average,
and was named *Golf Magazine*
Player of the Year. Recognized
for her consistency and power of concentration, Lopez
became the dominant player on the LPGA Tour, establishing a new record low-stroke average
at 70.73 in 1985. Today she remains one of the most popular players in the game, an outstanding
star who reached the LPGA Hall of Fame by the age of 30.

Ken Loeffler
NCAA Basketball Coach

"There are only two kinds of coaches — those who have been fired, and those who will be fired."

Jack Hurley
Boxing Promoter

"Looking at a fighter who can't punch is like kissing your brother-in-law."

Marriane Moore
Writer

"Fanaticism? No. Writing is exciting and baseball is like writing."

Pete Rose
Major League Outfielder
and Manager

"I'd go through hell

in a gasoline suit

to play baseball."

Nadia Comaneci
Gymnast and
Olympic Gold Medalist

"Hard work has

made it easy. That

is my secret. That

is why I win."

Steffi Graf
Champion Tennis Player

"As long as I can focus

on enjoying what I'm

doing, having fun, I

know I'll play well."

Earvin "Magic" Johnson
1959 –

A rare combination of size and speed, power and grace, Magic Johnson was a marvel on the basketball court. As a freshman at Michigan State University, he led the Spartans to their first Big Ten championship in nineteen years, as well as a National Collegiate Athletic Association title. In his rookie year in the National Basketball Association, he averaged eighteen points, ten rebounds, ten assists and three steals per game, topping off the season with a stunning performance in the finals against the Philadelphia 76ers, scoring forty-two points, shooting fourteen-for-twenty-three from the field, fourteen-for-fourteen from the free-throw line, with fifteen rebounds, seven assists and three steals. He was named the Playoff Most Valuable Player — the first rookie ever graced with the honor. In all, Magic garnered five NBA titles with the Lakers, two NBA All-Star MVP's, an NCAA championship, and two Olympic gold medals.

"I was given the gifts to become not only an athlete but also a businessman, a thinker who could help dispel the myth that most athletes are dumb jocks who can't see beyond the next game."

"I've had a great life. I've lived a life that no one could have imagined for me or anyone else."

"Off the floor I've always been Earvin; but in uniform I was Magic."

Woody Hayes
College Football Coach

"Anyone who will tear down sports will tear down America. Sports and religion have made America what it is today."

Casey Stengel
Major League Manager

"Good pitching will always stop good hitting, and vice versa."

Virginia Wade
Champion Tennis Player

"I always felt that I hadn't achieved what I wanted to achieve. I always felt I could get better. That's the whole incentive."

Mary Lou Retton
Gymnast and
Olympic Gold Medalist

"I like added pressure.

It makes me

work harder."

Mary Decker
Distance Runner

"I was born to be a

runner. I simply love

to run. It's almost like

the faster I go, the

easier it becomes."

Heywood Hale Broun
Writer

"Sports do not

build character.

They reveal it."

"When all is said and done, as a rule, more is said than done."

"I don't mind starting a season with unknowns. I just don't like finishing a season with a bunch of them."

"Coaching is nothing more than eliminating mistakes before you get fired."

Lou
Holtz

1937 –

As a young man, Lou Holtz was
content to dream the dreams of
small town life; his parents,
however, dreamed
bigger dreams
for him,
sending the
lackluster student
off to college. Little did
anyone know that he was to
become one of the most brilliant,
motivational coaches in the college
ranks. After a brief stint coaching in the
National Football League, he joined the University
of Arkansas and was named National Coach of the Year in
1977 and Southwestern Conference Coach of the Year in 1979.
Joining the University of Notre Dame in 1986, he led the Fighting
Irish to an undefeated season and a national championship in 1988,
rebuilding the reputation of the nation's most popular college team.

Walter Camp
College Football Coach

"When it comes to the football field, mind will always win over muscle and brute force."

Branch Rickey
Major League
Baseball Executive

"Problems are the price you pay for progress."

Joe Garagiola
Sports Broadcaster

"Players have hurts and fears and anxieties. As an announcer, I'm strictly for the underdog."

Stan Smith
Champion Tennis Player

"Experience tells you what to do; confidence allows you to do it."

Warren Spahn
Major League Pitcher

"Hitting is timing. Pitching is upsetting timing."

Lou Holtz
Head Coach,
University of Notre Dame

"If you burn your neighbor's house, it doesn't make your home look better."

Bobby Hull

1939 –

Bobby Hull handled the
puck with a precision that
was both uncommon and
unbelievable, with fairly
incredible results: in sixteen
NHL seasons, he scored 610 goals
and added 560 assists
in regular-season
games and produced
another sixty-two
goals and sixty-seven
assists in Stanley Cup play. He
was the first player to score more than
fifty goals in a season. He won the Art
Ross Trophy, awarded annually to the league's
leading scorer, three different times, the Hart
Trophy as the NHL's Most Valuable Player, twice, and
the Lady Bing Trophy, the symbol of large scoring numbers
combined with sportsmanship. For his contributions to the game of hockey, Hull was awarded
the Lester Patrick Trophy. He was voted to the All-Star team twelve times.

"Always keep your composure. You can't score from the penalty box; and to win, you have to score."

"Every professional athlete owes a debt of gratitude to the fans and management, and pays an installment every time he plays. He should never miss a payment."

"There is no better tonic for a hockey player than scoring a goal."

Jack Benny
Comedian

"Give me golf clubs, fresh air and a beautiful partner, and you can keep my golf clubs and the fresh air."

Russell Baker
Writer

"In America, it is sport that is the opiate of the masses."

Joe Paterno
College Football Coach and Athletic Director

"Besides pride, loyalty, discipline, heart and mind, confidence is the key to all the locks."

Fred Shero
Hockey Coach and
General Manager

"Experience is

the name we give

our mistakes."

Michelle McGann
LPGA Golfer

"I was always my

own person, not

ever really trying

to copy anybody."

Florence Griffith-Joyner
Sprinter and
Olympic Gold Medalist

"Young people need

positive role models. I

would like to be one."

"There's nothing that compares with the feeling of having accomplished something as a team, especially against the odds."

"I'll take a game-winning 1-yard plunge over a futile 90-yard breakaway any day."

"I want to be remembered as the guy who gave his all whenever he was on the field. I want people to know that Walter Payton will be putting out on every play."

Walter Payton

1954 –

He
was
called
"Sweetness" but
Walter Payton was one
of the most determined,
dominating and successful running
backs in the history of the National Football
League. He carried the ball more times for more yards than any other player. Over the course of
his thirteen-year career, he set a string of records that is staggering: most seasons rushing over 1,000
yards (10); most yards in a single game (275); receptions by a running back (486); consecutive
seasons with 1,000 yards or more (6); most yards carried (16,726); and consecutive seasons leading
the league in rushing (4). In 1985, Payton and the Chicago Bears were practically unbeatable;
only a loss to the Miami Dolphins marred a perfect season, a season that culminated with a resounding
46-10 victory over the New England Patriots in Super Bowl XX.

Steve McMichael
NFL Tackle

*"I think I'm going to
be remembered as one
of the craziest sons-of-
guns who ever came
down the pike, but
I play the game
with dignity."*

Tommy Lasorda
Major League Manager

*"The only way I'd
worry about the
weather is if it snows
on our side of the
field and not theirs."*

George Orwell
Writer

*"Serious sport has
nothing to do
with fair play."*

Greg Norman
PGA Golfer

"I'm a very intense person. When I go after something, I want to go after it with everything I have. I want to push myself to the edge."

Chuck Knox
NFL Coach

"Practice without improvement is meaningless."

Roy Campanella
Major League Catcher

"You gotta be a man to play baseball for a living, but you gotta have a lot of little boy in you, too."

Mildred "Babe" Didrikson Zaharias

1914 – 1956

A tall and slender woman of enormous ability, Mildred "Babe" Didrikson Zaharias is considered the greatest female athlete of all time. She dominated women's sports in America for more than a quarter of a century with an overwhelming combination of raw power, agility and natural talent. She was an accomplished baseball player, a world-class diver, swimmer, an Olympic silver medalist in the high jump, and a gold medalist in the javelin and eighty-meter low hurdles. She helped found the Ladies Professional Golf Association after winning seventeen consecutive amateur tournaments, and went on to dominate the LPGA Tour by winning ten major championships, including three U.S. Open championships and four Western Opens. She was chosen "Athlete of the Half Century" by the Associated Press in 1950.

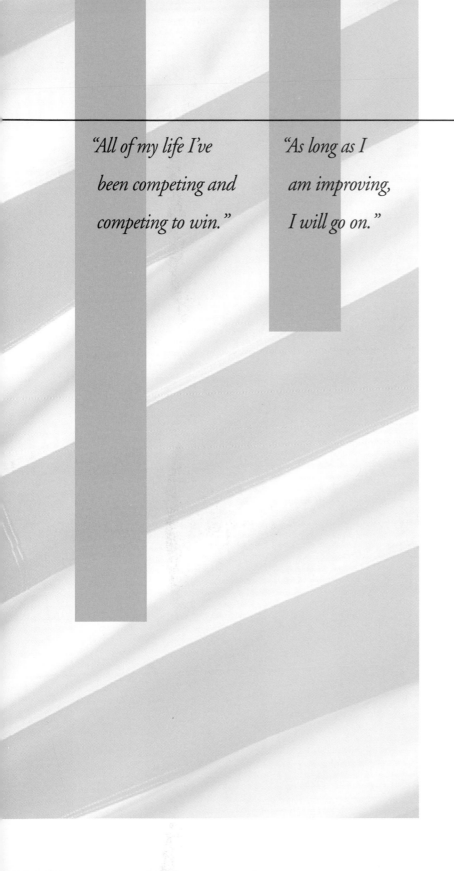

"All of my life I've been competing and competing to win."

"As long as I am improving, I will go on."

"I don't seem able to do my best unless I'm behind or in trouble."

Joe Paterno
College Football Coach
and Athletic Director

"Publicity is like

poison. It doesn't

hurt unless you

swallow it."

Bob Hope
Comedian

"If you watch a game,

it's fun. If you play it,

it's recreation. If you

work at it, it's golf."

Sebastian Coe
Distance Runner and
Olympic Gold Medalist

"All pressure is self-

inflicted. It's what

you make of it —

or how you let it

rub off on you."

Evonne Goolagong
Champion Tennis Player

"When everybody said I'd never be any good again, it just made me push on."

Chuck Mills
College Football Coach

"Some coaches pray for wisdom. I pray for 260-pound tackles."

David Feherty
PGA Golfer

"It's how you deal with failure that determines how you achieve success."

"During my 18 years I came to bat almost 109,000 times. I struck out about 1,700 times and walked maybe 1,800 times. You figure a ballplayer will average about 500 at-bats a season. That means I played seven years in the major leagues without even hitting the ball."

"To play ball was all I lived for."

"I'd go back to making $100,000 a year in a second if I could play ball again."

Mickey Mantle

1931 –

Mickey Mantle was the most feared hitter in baseball, a devastating player who could hit tape-measure home runs from either side of the plate. Replacing the legendary Joe DiMaggio in 1952, his nearly limitless talents led the New York Yankees to twelve fall classics in fourteen years, including seven World Championships. He established World Series records for most home runs, runs batted in, runs and bases on balls. In 1956, one of his finest seasons, Mantle hit 52 home runs with 130 RBI and a .353 batting average to win the Triple Crown. He also led the league with 132 runs, a .705 slugging percentage and 112 walks, capping the year with the first of his three Most Valuable Player awards.

Bill Bradley
U.S. Senator and
NBA Forward

"The taste of defeat

has a richness

of experience

all its own."

Hubert Green
PGA Golfer

"Winning breeds

confidence and

confidence breeds

winning."

Nick Niccolau
NFL Coach

"Our trainer has

become so injury

conscious that he is

putting life jackets

on the players before

he allows them in

the whirlpool."

Don Hutson
NFL Offensive End

"For every pass I ever caught in a game, I caught a thousand in practice."

Mark Twain
Writer

"There is no use in your walking five miles to fish when you can depend on being as unsuccessful near home."

Bill Foster
NCAA Basketball Coach

"There's no letter 'I' in the word teamwork."

Muhammad Ali

1942 –

With his flawless reflexes, punishing power and remarkable speed, Cassius Clay was destined to become one of the most celebrated professional fighters of all time. Making his championship debut in 1964, Clay, who made his first and last title fight under that name before changing it to Muhammad Ali according to Muslim custom, defeated Sonny Liston in a technical knock out. Over the next fifteen years, Ali elevated the sport of boxing to new levels of popularity, becoming only the second man in history to recapture the heavyweight championship. Ali reigned for three more years before losing the title — only to regain it again seven months later for an unprecedented third time.

"There are no pleasures in a fight, but some of my fights have been a pleasure to win."

"You could be the world's best garbage man, the world's best model; it doesn't matter what you do if you're the best."

"Age is whatever you think it is. You are as old as you think you are."

Billy Martin
Major League Second
Baseman and Manager

*"When you're a
winner, you come
back no matter
what happened the
day before."*

Joe Robbie
Owner, Miami Dolphins

*"There is no substitute
for effort. Always
play up to your full
potential in every
endeavor. The greatest
extravagance of
all is to waste
human potential."*

Tom Watson
PGA Golfer

*"I was not a winner
when I first came out
on the tour. I had to
develop a trust in
myself that I had the
ability to win."*

Gale Sayers
NFL Running Back

"If you don't have enough pride, you're going to get your butt beat every play."

Mark Spitz
Swimmer and
Olympic Gold Medalist

"I'm trying to do the best I can. I'm not concerned about tomorrow, but with what goes on today."

Lefty Gomez
Major League Pitcher

"We lost 14 straight. Then we had a game rained out and it felt so good we threw a victory dinner."

54

"If you aren't fired with enthusiasm, you will be fired with enthusiasm."

"Coaches who can outline plays on a blackboard are a dime a dozen. The ones who win get inside their players and motivate."

"Winning isn't everything, but wanting to win is."

Vince
Lombardi

1913 – 1970

When Vince Lombardi accepted the head coaching position at Green Bay, he inherited a team of aging veterans and fresh rookies — and created one of the most dominating teams in National Football League history. He was strict but fair, and he accepted nothing less than the absolute best from his players. And they responded. His motivational techniques have been heralded for generating success inside and outside the world of sports. Among NFL coaches, his winning percentage of 74 percent remains an unparalleled standard. In a seven-year span, his Packers won five NFL championships, providing dominating victories in the first two Super Bowls.

Howard Cosell
Sports Broadcaster

"Sports is the

toy department

of human life."

Casey Stengel
Major League Manager

"Managing is getting

paid for home runs

someone else hits."

Nick Faldo
PGA Golfer

"The word is control.

That's my ultimate —

to have control."

Andre Agassi
Champion Tennis Player

"I've realized my dreams of winning a Grand Slam tournament. If my career was over tomorrow, I got more than I deserved, than I could ever ask for."

Don Carter
Champion Bowler

"One of the advantages bowling has over golf is that you seldom lose a bowling ball."

Lawrence Taylor
NFL Linebacker

"There are guys who want to shoot the last shot, and others who want to pass off. I want that last shot."

Jimmy Connors
1952 –

For more than two decades, the
seemingly ageless Jimmy
Connors sent
his two-
fisted
backhand
roaring across the net
with startling precision.
His powerful baseline style
earned him the number-one
ranking in the world for five
consecutive years. Considered feisty
and controversial in his early days on the circuit,
he became the grand old man of tennis, earning
the respect and admiration of both the public and
the media. In all, Connors was ranked in the U.S.
Top Ten a record 20 times during his twenty-one year professional career. He was the all-time
leader in professional singles titles and matches won at both the U.S. Open and Wimbledon.

"I hate to lose more than I like to win. I hate to see the happiness on their faces when they beat me."

"The problem is that when you get experience, you're too damned old to do anything about it."

"I don't want to hear about number two. There's only one number one. It's not a matter of money — just pride — pure and simple. I want to be the best."

Bob Devaney
College Football Coach

"I had a friend with a lifetime contract. After two bad years the university president called him into his office and pronounced him dead."

Julie Krone
Jockey

"With racing, you never rest on your laurels, and there are no counterfeits."

Samuel Johnson
Essayist and Writer

"Angling — I can only compare to a stick and string, with a worm at one end and a fool at the other."

Lefty Gomez
Major League Pitcher

"I'm throwing twice as hard as I used to but the ball isn't going as fast."

Kareem Abdul-Jabbar
NBA Center

"One man can be a crucial ingredient on a team, but one man cannot make a team."

Roger Staubach
NFL Quarterback and Sports Broadcaster

"Confidence is the result of hours and days and weeks and years of constant work and dedication."

"I just try to concentrate on concentrating."

"You have to want to win and expect that you are going to win. Top players have that edge."

"I hope, when I stop, people will think that somehow I mattered."

Martina Navratilova

1956 –

In 1978, at the age of twenty-one, Martina Navratilova captured her first title at Wimbledon. Days later, she was ranked the top player in women's tennis for the first time as well. With a blistering serve and a rock-solid groundstroke, the left-handed Navratilova would emerge as the dominant player in women's tennis throughout the last half of the nineteen-eighties. She captured her record ninth Wimbledon title in 1990, and at one point won seventy-four consecutive matches over eleven months and thirteen tournaments. In all, Navratilova has won 18 Grand Slam singles titles — including six straight — and 37 Grand Slam doubles titles. She is the all-time women's leader in singles titles and money won.

Leo Durocher
Major League Manager

"'How you play the game is for college boys.' When you're playing for money, winning is the only thing that counts."

Bruce Jenner
Decathlete and
Olympic Gold Medalist

"I learned that the only way you are going to get anywhere in life is to work hard at it. If you do, you'll win — if you don't, you won't."

Miller Barber
PGA Golfer

"I don't say my golf game is bad, but if I grew tomatoes, they'd come up sliced."

Billy Tubbs
NCAA Basketball Coach

"This year we plan to run and shoot. Next season we hope to run and score."

Fred Shero
Hockey Coach and General Manager

"I'm like a duck: Calm above water, but paddling like hell underneath."

Jack Roper
Heavyweight Boxer

"I zigged when I should have zagged."

Joe Montana
1956 –

After leading the University of Notre Dame to the national title in 1977, Joe Montana was drafted by the San Francisco 49ers, a team that had never been to a Super Bowl. By the close of the season in 1989, they had played in four Super Bowls — and had won them all. Considered by many to be the finest quarterback in the history of the National Football League, Montana dissected defenses with surgeon-like precision. Ranked in the top ten in all-time passing efficiency, yards passing and touchdown passes, he earned back-to-back regular season Most Valuable Player honors in 1989 and 1990. Even more remarkable, he is the only three-time Super Bowl MVP in the history of the NFL.

"Confidence is a very fragile thing. Just because you have it in college doesn't mean you're gonna have it in the pros."

"Me, a Notre Dame legend? I go to the store, buy milk, and forget the bread. I try to hammer a nail and hit my thumb. Do legends do that?"

"I'll take my job over my wife's job of raising our children — because hers is tougher."

Wilt Chamberlain
NBA Center
(Discussing Coach
  Alex Hannum's
  training sessions)

"If I can miss five

minutes of one of his

practices, I feel like

I am adding five

years to my life."

William Perry
NFL Tackle

"When I was little,

I was big."

Leo Durocher
Major League Manager

"You don't save a

pitcher for tomorrow.

Tomorrow it

may rain."

Bill Vaughan
Writer

"As a nation we are dedicated to keeping physically fit — and parking as close to the stadium as possible."

Satchel Paige
Major League Pitcher

"Don't look back. Someone might be gaining on you."

Theodore Roosevelt
24th President of the United States

"In life, as in a football game, the principle to follow is: Hit the line hard."

"If you are caught on a golf course during a storm and are afraid of lightning, hold up a one-iron. Not even God can hit a one-iron."

"My wife doesn't care what I do when I'm away — as long as I don't enjoy myself."

"There's no such thing as natural touch. Touch is something you create by hitting millions of golf balls."

Lee Trevino

1939 –

When he defeated the legendary
Jack Nicklaus by four strokes at the
U.S. Open at Oak Hill in 1968,
Lee Trevino captured the attention
of the golfing world with his
unorthodox character and
entertaining style. But
although the stars
did not always
approve of his nonstop
jokes and running chatter,
they respected his magical
skills on the fairways and his brilliant golf-
course strategy — as well as his uncanny
ability to bring in the spectators. During
his professional career, Trevino was a
two-time winner of three major
championships — the U.S. Open, the British Open and the PGA. After twenty-seven victories
on the PGA Tour, he went on to become one of the leading celebrities on the U.S. Senior Tour.
PGA Player of the Year in 1971, he entered the World Golf Hall of Fame in 1981.

Buzzy Bavasi
Baseball Executive

*"We live by the
Golden Rule. Those
who have the gold
make the rules."*

Sam Snead
PGA Golfer

*"Forget your
opponents; always
play against par."*

Sugar Ray Leonard
Boxer and
Sports Broadcaster

*"My ambition is not to
be just a good fighter.
I want to be great,
something special."*

Peggy Fleming
Figure Skater and
Olympic Gold Medalist

"The most important thing is to love your sport. Never do it to please someone else. It has to be yours."

Dizzy Dean
Major League Pitcher

"The Good Lord was good to me. He gave me a strong body, a good right arm, and a weak mind."

Joe Gibbs
NFL Head Coach

"People who enjoy what they are doing invariably do it well."

John Wooden

1910 –

As a senior at Purdue University, John Wooden set a Big Ten scoring record, led Purdue to a national championship, and won College Player of the Year honors. After his days in the National Basketball Association, he settled in Los Angeles as head basketball coach with the University of California. There, throughout the sixties and seventies, Wooden and his Bruins established a series of records that may never be broken: eighty-eight consecutive victories; ten National Collegiate Athletic Association titles, including seven consecutive crowns; thirty-eight straight NCAA tournament victories and eight straight undefeated conference championships. Elected to the Basketball Hall of Fame as a player, Wooden was also so honored as a coach — the only man to be recognized in both fields.

"It's not so important who starts the game, but who finishes it."

"Class is an intangible quality which commands, rather than demands, the respect of others."

"It's what you learn after you know it all that counts."

Reggie Jackson
Major League Outfielder

"The will to win is worthless if you don't get paid for it."

Janet Evans
Swimmer and
Olympic Gold Medalist

"On the starting block before my first Olympic race, I was smiling, because I was having fun. That's what it is all about, to have fun."

JoAnne Carner
LPGA Golfer

"Money was never a goal for me because of my amateur training. I was taught to win and that was it."

Charles O. Finley
Owner,
Oakland Athletics

"Sweat plus sacrifice equals success."

Vin Scully
Sports Broadcaster

"It's a mere moment in a man's life between an All-Star Game and an Old-Timers' Game."

Willie Shoemaker
Jockey

"I've always believed that anybody with a little ability, a little guts and the desire to apply himself can make it."

"Basketball is my escape, my refuge. It seems that everything else is so... so busy and complicated."

"I've always tried to project everything positive. People say you need role models in the world, and people were asking for them, and I never thought a role model should be negative."

"The game is my wife. It demands loyalty and responsibility, and it gives me back fulfillment and peace."

Michael Jordan

1963 –

When it came to grace
and style on the
basketball
court,
one player was
truly in a league of his own.
The skywalking, above-the-rim
skills of Michael Jordan made him the
dominating player in the National Basketball
Association throughout his career — and the most recognized athlete in the world. His list of
achievements is nothing short of breathtaking: College Player of the Year; two-time Olympic gold
medalist; seven-time All-NBA 1st team; three-time regular season Most Valuable Player; three-
time MVP of the NBA Finals; and NBA All-Star Game MVP. In a sport of stars and superstars,
Michael Jordan was the most awesomely gifted and competitive player of all time.

Pop Warner
College Football Coach

"You play the way

you practice."

Joe Torre
Major League First
Baseman and Manager

"I'm not sure whether

I'd rather be

managing or testing

bulletproof vests."

Richard M. Nixon
37th President of the
United States

"If I had my life to

live all over again,

I'd have ended up

a sportswriter."

Julius Erving
NBA Forward

"I keep both eyes on my man. The basket hasn't moved on me yet."

Joe Louis
Heavyweight Boxer

"He can run, but he can't hide."

Vernon Law
Major League Pitcher

"Experience is a hard teacher because she gives the test first, the lesson afterwards."

Wilma Rudolph

1940 –

Miraculously, within four years of recovering from disabling bouts with pneumonia and scarlet fever, Wilma Rudolph became a superstar in both basketball and track, tying for first place in the 200-meter dash in the Olympic trials in 1956. After winning a bronze medal in the 400-meter relay in Melbourne that year — as well as the Sullivan Award, an honor given annually to America's outstanding athlete — Rudolph set her sights on the 1960 Olympics. There, in a stunning performance that made her the most celebrated Olympian in Rome, she won gold medals in the 400-meter relay and the 100- and 200-meter dashes — one of only three women to sweep the three sprint events.

"I would be very disappointed if I were only remembered as a runner because I feel that my contribution to the youth in America has far exceeded the woman who was the Olympic champion. The challenge is still there."

"My interests are my family and the kids I'm working with. I'm trying to develop champions."

"My mother taught me very early to believe I could achieve any accomplishment I wanted to. The first was to walk without braces."

Pat Day
Jockey

"I know there's a Derby out there with my name on it."

Jerry Glanville
NFL Head Coach

"If you're a pro coach, NFL stands for Not For Long."

Steve Garvey
Major League
First Baseman

"You have to set the goals that are almost out of reach. If you set a goal that is attainable without much work or thought, you are stuck with something below your true talent and potential."

Erma Bombeck
Comedian

"If a man watches three football games in a row, he should be declared legally dead."

Charlie Gehringer
Major League
Second Baseman

"Ball players do things backward. First we play, then we retire and go to work."

Jack Thompson
NFL Quarterback

"It's amazing what the human body can do when chased by a bigger human body."

"You learn how to be a gracious winner and an understanding loser."

"When you have confidence, you can have a lot of fun; and when you have fun, you can do amazing things."

"To be a leader, you have to make people want to follow you, and nobody wants to follow someone who doesn't know where he's going."

Joe
Namath

1943 –

A brash and colorful competitor,
Joe Namath led his New York
Jets to the Super Bowl in 1969 in
what appeared to be the mismatch
of the century against the
dominating Baltimore Colts.
In some circles, the
Colts were favored to
win by as many as 45
points. Yet a week before the big
showdown Namath guaranteed
victory — then went on to fulfill his
promise with a brilliant performance
against a surprised Baltimore team. For his
heroic efforts, Namath was voted the Most Valuable
Player of Super Bowl III. Voted twice to the all-AFL
team, he was also voted all-NFL in 1972. He was
elected to the Pro Football Hall of Fame in 1985.

Bonnie Blair
Speedskater and
Olympic Gold Medalist

"My parents put skates on me at age two, the way it should be if you're serious, and I've always liked it."

Leo Durocher
Major League Manager

"Nice guys finish last."

Bud Wilkinson
NFL Head Coach

"You can motivate players better with kind words than you can with a whip."

Mario Andretti
Race Car Driver

"Desire is the key to motivation, but it's the determination and commitment to an unrelenting pursuit of your goal, a commitment to excellence, that will enable you to attain the success you seek."

Bo Jackson
NFL Running Back and
Major League Outfielder

"I'll never worry about not being successful. I'll just take it one day at a time and play the best I can."

Lefty Gomez
Major League Pitcher

"The secret of my success is clean living and a fast outfield."

Joe DiMaggio

1914 –

A man of quiet grace and style, Joe DiMaggio made history in 1941 by hitting safely in fifty-six consecutive games, a sustained effort many experts consider the most remarkable achievement in all of sports. During a career interrupted for three years by World War II, DiMaggio hit 361 home runs, drove in 1,537 runs, posted one of the best-ever slugging percentages at .571, and compiled a .325 career batting average. He roamed the vast center field of Yankee Stadium with ease and confidence, and charged the base paths with speed and intelligence. In all, DiMaggio led the New York Yankees to ten World Series titles in thirteen seasons, leading the league in home runs, runs batted in, and batting average twice each. He was voted the league's Most Valuable Player three times.

"A ball player's got to be kept hungry to become a big leaguer. That's why no boy from a rich family ever made the big leagues."

"Live in hope and die in despair."

"A person always doing his or her best becomes a natural leader, just by example."

Rick Mears
Race Car Driver

"There's nothing quite like Pole Day at Indy. The pressure is so intense. You have to do four perfect laps. The race is a piece of cake by comparison: You have 500 miles to get it right."

Damon Runyon
Writer

"The race is not always to the swift nor the battle to the strong — but that's the way to bet it."

Bob Cousy
NBA Guard

"Michael Jordan goes up, stops for a cup of coffee, looks over the scenery, then follows through with a tomahawk jam."

Yogi Berra
Major League Catcher
and Manager

"So I'm ugly. So what?

I never saw anyone

hit with his face."

Gary Player
PGA Golfer

"If I had to choose

between my wife

and my putter, well,

I'd miss her."

Brian Bosworth
NFL Linebacker

"If you can miss getting

up in the morning

and running into

a wall, I miss

playing football."

94

"When you make a mistake, there are only three things you should ever do about it:
1. Admit it
2. Learn from it, and
3. Don't repeat it."

"Winning isn't everything, but it beats anything that comes in second."

"The competition in the job market today calls for being as well-prepared as possible. You must prepare for your future and that key is education."

Paul "Bear" Bryant

1913 – 1983

He began his coaching career at the University of Maryland in 1945, went on to Kentucky, then Texas A&M before settling in at Alabama. For the next quarter of a century, Bear Bryant coached the "Crimson Tide," guiding the likes of future professional quarterbacks Joe Namath, Ken Stabler and Richard Todd. He understood, possibly more than any other college coach, the importance of encouraging the individual while building the team. He led Alabama to five national championships and fifteen bowl wins, including eight Sugar Bowls. When he died in 1983 at the age of 69, just four weeks after his last victory and six weeks after announcing his retirement, his 323-85-17 record made him the all-time winning coach in college football history.

Cal Ripken Jr.
Major League Shortstop

"I never perceived myself to be the big star. I'm only one of nine guys. I think it is good to think that way."

Bo Jackson
NFL Running Back and
Major League Outfielder

"If my doctor says I can play, believe me, you'll see me out there getting the guts kicked out of me, or me kicking the guts out of somebody else."

Rodney Dangerfield
Comedian

"I went to a fight the other night and a hockey game broke out."

Eric Dickerson
NFL Running Back

"If I've lost a step, it's a step a lot of other guys never had."

Isiah Thomas
NBA Guard

"If all I'm remembered for is being a good basketball player, then I've done a bad job with the rest of my life."

Casey Stengel
Major League Manager

"I was not successful as a ball player, as it was a game of skill."

Jack Nicklaus

1940 –

Jack Nicklaus is the most influential and arguably the finest golfer of all time. He captured the U.S. Open in 1962 and the Masters twenty-four years later, marking the longest stretch between first and last major titles in any sports career. With nearly one hundred tour victories worldwide, including twenty major championships, his record is nothing short of astonishing. His victories include two U.S. Amateurs, four U.S. Opens, three British Opens, five PGA Championships and a record six Masters.

"The one strongest, most important idea in my game of golf— my cornerstone — is that I want to be the best. I wouldn't accept anything less than that. My ability to concentrate and work toward that goal has been my greatest asset."

"It's great to win, but it's also great fun just to be in the thick of any truly well and hard-fought contest against opponents you respect, whatever the outcome."

(When asked why he tees up his ball so high)
"Through the years of experience I have found that air offers less resistance than dirt."

Roger Maris
Major League Outfielder

"I'll never take abuse from anybody, big or small, important or unimportant, if I think it's undeserved."

Maureen Connolly
Champion Tennis Player

"Tennis can be a grind and there is always the danger of going stale if you think about it too much. You have to be able to relax between matches and tournaments."

Stirling Moss
Race Car Driver

"To achieve anything in this game, you must be prepared to dabble on the boundary of disaster."

Bobby Nichols
PGA Golfer

"If you've got to remind yourself to concentrate during competition, you've got no chance to concentrate."

Jackie Robinson
Major League
Second Baseman

"Many people resented my impatience and honesty, but I never cared about acceptance as much as I cared about respect."

Bryant Gumbel
Sports Broadcaster

"The other sports are just sports. Baseball is a love."

"I believe in women.
I believe in myself.
I believe in my body."

"Whatever muscles
I have are the
product of my
own hard work —
nothing else."

"I can feel the wind go
by when I run. It feels
good. It feels fast."

Evelyn Ashford

1957 –

Blistering speed and a deep desire to win earned Evelyn Ashford a place on five consecutive Olympic teams. At a time when the East German women dominated the sprint, Ashford set her sights on regaining the gold for the United States. In addition to being an enormously talented runner, she was also a tireless worker, spending hour after hour sharpening her skills and improving her technique. Her no-nonsense, work-is-first method proved very effective; when the time came for her to perform, she excelled. Ashford won four Olympic gold medals — the 100 meter in 1984, and the 4x100 meter in 1984, 1988 and 1982 — as well as a silver medal in the 100 meter in 1988.

Scottie Pippen
NBA Forward

"I've always led by example and I'm not that vocal."

Tommy Lasorda
Major League Manager

"I've learned that the only way to get respect from people is to give them respect — and that's my way of doing it."

Ben Crenshaw
PGA Golfer

"Golf is the hardest game in the world. There's no way you can ever get it. Just when you think you do, the game jumps up and puts you in your place."

Baron Pierre DeConbertin
Founder,
Modern Olympic Games

"The important thing in the Olympic Games is not to win but to take part; the important thing in life is not the triumph but the struggle. The essential thing is not to have conquered but to have fought well."

Paul Brown
NFL Coach

"A winner never whines."

Joe Louis
Heavyweight Boxer

"Every man's got to figure to get beat sometime."

Knute Rockne

1888 – 1931

A persuasive and charismatic leader, Knute Rockne understood the dynamics of motivation better than any man in the Golden Age of Sports. It was during a fiercely contested battle against Army in 1928 that he inspired his Notre Dame team to victory with the most romantic episode in the history of college football, the tale of a man named George Gipp, who got off a sick bed in the dead of winter to take the field one wind-blustered icy day — simply for the love of the game. "Win one for the Gipper" may be the most well-known rallying cry in sporting history, a legendary story from a legendary man. When Knute Rockne was killed in a plane crash in 1931, he had led his Fighting Irish to three consecutive national championships, posted a record of 105-12-5 and built a winning percentage, .881, that may never be surpassed.

"One man practicing sportsmanship is far better than a hundred teaching it."

"Football is a game played with the arms, legs, and shoulders — but mostly from the neck up."

"The secret of winning football games is working more as a team, less as individuals. I play not my 11 best, but my best 11."

Emory Jones
St. Louis Blues
Arena Manager

"Hockey players are like mules. They have no fear of punishment and no hope of reward."

Bruce Jenner
Decathlete and
Olympic Gold Medalist

"An athlete has such a narrow view of life he does not know reality."

Roger Maris
Major League Outfielder

"…I do know that when I'm not hitting, my wife could pitch and get me out."

Max Baer
Heavyweight Boxer

"If you ever get belted and see three fighters through a haze, go after the one in the middle. That's what ruined me — I went after the two guys on the end."

Bum Phillips
NFL Head Coach

"The only discipline that lasts is self-discipline."

John Bach
NBA Coach

"Defense starts with a determination and pride to excel. It comes with knowledge and communication and you've got to have heart. To the timid soul nothing is possible. To the aggressor, everything is possible."

"*I always know what's happening on the court. I see a situation occur and I respond.*"

"*I really don't like talking about money. All I can say is that the Good Lord must have wanted me to have it.*"

"*Push yourself again and again. Don't give an inch until the final buzzer sounds.*"

Larry Bird

1956 –

His command of the court was so complete his teammates never ceased to marvel at the creativity he displayed season after season —but most especially during the pressure-packed Play Offs. When Larry Bird arrived in the National Basketball Association in 1979, the Boston Celtics were one of the worst teams in basketball. By 1981 they were the best — beating the Houston Rockets for the NBA Championship. Bird led the Celtics to titles in 1984 and 1986 as well. Individually, he gathered three consecutive Most Valuable Player awards — from 1984 through 1986, only the third player in NBA history to be so honored — was voted Play Off MVP twice, and led the U.S. Olympic Dream Team to gold in 1992.

Sugar Ray Robinson
Middleweight Boxer

"Boxing is the art of self-defense. You have to pattern your style for each fight against the style of the man you're fighting."

Virginia Wade
Champion Tennis Player

"Winners aren't popular. Losers often are."

Casey Stengel
Major League Manager
(Reflecting on the
New York Yankees)

"I'll say this. This is the greatest ball club a man could manage. Certainly the best I've ever known. I am indebted to them for the way they came through for me. They won it, not me."

John Brodie
NFL Quarterback

"There is an intensity and a danger in football — as in life generally — which keeps us alive and awake. It is a test of our awareness and ability. Like so much of life, it presents us with the choice of responding either with fear or with action."

Wayne Gretzky
NHL Center

"I love playing and I enjoy the thrill of competing. The better the team plays, the better you play."

Roger Bannister
Distance Runner

"Without the concentration of the mind and the will, performance would not result."

Babe Ruth

1895 – 1948

Decades after his final appearance at home plate, the name of Babe Ruth is still spoken with admiration and affection. He is the stuff of legends, baseball's quintessential slugger. Until the time of Hank Aaron, Ruth's accomplishments seemed unapproachable — 714 home runs and 2,211 runs batted in. And though he ranks second to Aaron in the record books in both categories today, he hit more home runs more often than any other man. He averaged one home run for every 11.76 at-bats, compared to Aaron who managed only one home run every 16.38 trips to the plate. Ruth also remains the leader in slugging percentage, at .690 — once posting an .847 single-season slugging percentage, the highest ever — and bases on balls, at 2,056. More importantly, when people speak of accomplishments of epic proportions in any life endeavor, they inevitably mention Babe Ruth.

"You just can't beat the person who never gives up."

"A part of control is learning to correct your weaknesses. The person doesn't live who was born with everything."

"The way a team plays as a whole determines its success."

Matt Biondi
Swimmer and
Olympic Gold Medalist

"There is too much emphasis on success and failure, and too little on how a person grows as he works. Enjoy the journey, enjoy every moment and quit worrying about winning and losing."

Bill Fitch
NBA Coach

"I'm independently wealthy. I have enough money to last me the rest of my life — provided I die tomorrow."

Julie Krone
Jockey
(after becoming the
first female to win
the Belmont Stakes)

"I have fifteen bouquets, about 50 cards and 500 phone calls. It's as if you put all the people in my life in one pot, stirred them all up and pulled them all out one by one."

Mario Andretti
Race Car Driver

"Circumstances may cause interruptions and delays, but never lose sight of your goal. Prepare yourself in every way you can by increasing your knowledge and adding to your experience, so that you can make the most of opportunity when it occurs."

Bob Richards
Pole Vaulter

"Show me a boy or girl with a desire to win, and I'll show you a person who will work hard the thousands of hours it takes to win. If they lack desire, they won't work."

Lou Groza
NFL Lineman

"Old placekickers never die, they just go on missing the point."

"A champion is afraid of losing. Everyone else is afraid of winning."

(Characterizing the sport of tennis) "A perfect combination of violent action taking place in an atmosphere of total tranquility."

"Certain people helping in certain sports. Certain sports are made for certain people — every athlete must find the sport for which he or she is best suited."

Billie Jean King

1943 –

When Billie Jean King soundly defeated the self-proclaimed male chauvinist Bobby Riggs in an exhibition tennis match televised around the world, she bolstered the cause of women's rights and ignited public interest in championship tennis. A graceful stylist on the court, King was the singles champion at Wimbledon on six separate occasions. She was the U.S. champion four times and, with her victory at the Virginia Slims-Thunderbird tournament at Phoenix, she became the first woman professional — and the first woman athlete in history — to earn $100,000 during a single competitive year.

Tommy Lasorda
Major League Manager

"Managing is like holding a dove in your hand. Squeeze too hard and you kill it; not hard enough and it flies away."

Bo Jackson
NFL Running Back and Major League Outfielder

"Regardless of whether I hit a 440-foot home run or strike out, the game will always be fun. All I want is to be able to get in some quality cuts every at-bat."

Paul O'Neil
Writer

"The art of running the mile consists in essence of reaching the threshold of unconsciousness at the instant of breasting the tape."

Other Titles Available from Successories® Library

Great Quotes from Great Leaders
The Best of Success
Great Quotes from Great Women
Never Never Quit
Motivation Lombardi Style
Quality, Service, Teamwork & The Quest for Excellence
Your Attitude Determines Your Altitude
Opportunity Selling
Customer Care
Motivational Quotes
Commitment to Quality
Humorous Quotes from the Business World
Zig Ziglar's Favorite Quotations
Winning with Teamwork
The Power of Goals
Management Magic
Innovation & Creativity
Pride
Motivational Minutes
The Wit & Wisdom of Our American Presidents

TOLL FREE (800) 535-2773
919 Springer Drive • Lombard, IL 60148